The Seven
Churches of Asia

Robert Murray M'Cheyne

Christian Focus Publications

Christian Focus Publications publishes biblically-accurate books for adults and children. The books in the adult range are published in three imprints.

Christian Heritage contains classic writings from the past.

Christian Focus contains popular works including biographies, commentaries, doctrine, and Christian living.

Mentor focuses on books written at a level suitable for Bible College and seminary students, pastors, and others; the imprint includes commentaries, doctrinal studies, examination of current issues, and church history.

For a free catalogue of all our titles, please write to
Christian Focus Publications,
Geanies House, Fearn,
Ross-shire, IV20 1TW, Great Britain

For details of our titles visit us on our web site
http://www.christianfocus.com

Christian Focus Publications,
Geanies House, Fearn, Ross-shire,
IV20 1TW, Great Britain

Cover design by Owen Daily

Contents

EXPOSITION 1

The Church in Ephesus

Unto the angel of the church of Ephesus write; These things saith He that holdeth the seven stars in His right hand, who walketh in the midst of the seven golden candlesticks; I know thy works, and thy labour, and thy patience, and how thou canst not bear them which are evil: and thou hast tried them which say they are apostles, and are not, and hast found them liars: and hast borne, and hast patience, and for my name's sake hast laboured, and hast not fainted. Nevertheless I have somewhat against thee, because thou hast left thy first love. Remember therefore from whence thou art fallen, and repent, and do the first works; or else I will come unto thee quickly, and will remove thy candlestick out of his place, except thou repent. But this thou hast, that thou hatest the deeds of the Nicolaitans, which I also hate. He that hath an ear, let him hear what the Spirit saith unto the churches; To him that overcometh will I give to eat of the tree of life, which is in the midst of the paradise of God (Rev. 2:1-7).

In the second and third chapters of the Revelation are written Seven Epistles to the Seven Churches of Asia; and they are sweet, because they show us not only what the mind of Christ *was*, but what *it is*, now that He is in glory.

The gospels are very sweet, because they show us what the mind of Christ was in the days of His flesh, when He tabernacled with men upon earth; but *these* are sweet, because they show us that Jesus is the same when standing at the right hand of the Father, as when He stood by the Sea of Galilee; that He is the same now while holding the reins of the universe, as when He stood by His disciples, and, blessing them, said, 'Blessed be ye poor: for yours is the kingdom of God.'

This epistle is to the Church of Ephesus, the chief of the churches of Asia – the church to which Paul went twice-where he remained for three years – and where he left Timothy. Let us see.

In what character Christ is mentioned here.
He is said to be holding the seven stars in His right hand, and walking in the midst of the seven golden candlesticks. First, he holdeth the seven stars in His right hand; these stars are His ministers. Now, the right hand is the place of power; ministers only shine as long as they are in the hand of Christ. People now look too much to ministers; they expect to get wisdom from them; but we are not put up to be between you and Christ. As I have told you before, the only use of the pole was to hold up the brazen serpent. No one thought of looking at the pole: so are we here to hold up Christ in the sight of you all; we are to give testimony to the truth; we are witnesses for Christ; we are to hold up Jesus before you, and before ourselves too: so that we shall disappear, and nothing shall be seen but Christ. The star of Bethlehem led the wise men, and stood over the place where the young child lay; so are we to be the star, to lead you to the place where the young child lies. The morning star goes out when the sun appears, and many stars go out when the soul has been led to the Sun.

And, second, 'Jesus walketh in the midst of the seven golden candlesticks.' He walketh in the midst of the churches; He is in this church this night. 'Go ye into all the world.' What, Lord! Shall we go in among these wicked people? Shall we leave Thee, and go into that dazzling, into that cruel world? Yes, but 'lo, I am with you always, even unto the end of the world.' This is what Christ said upon earth, but perhaps He does not say this now. Yes, He walked in the midst of the golden candlesticks when on earth, and He walketh in the midst of them still. Jesus walketh in the midst of believers; they are the candlesticks; they were once of cast metal, but, united to Christ, they become gold, pure gold. What little Samuel did, was to walk among the candlesticks, and see that they were kept burning: so doth Christ; He walketh in the midst of believers, to preserve them, to see that they burn, to pour in fresh oil, to give the Holy Spirit. If you were to put a lamp in a place where there was no air, it would go out; and yet, how is it that believers are kept in this world? It takes all the power of God to do it; it takes all power, in heaven and in earth; but He is able, and He will do it. They would soon grow dim but He will keep them burning.

What Christ says in the praise of Ephesus. 'I know thy works.' It is Jesus that knows them.

Now, does this make you quake – does it make you fear – does it make you tremble from head to foot, to think that the eye of Christ is upon you, that He says, I know thy works? Why should it? Because when Jesus says to you, I know thy sin; you should say to Him, I know Thy sufferings. When He says to you, I know all thy wants, that thou hast many; then you should say to Him, I know Thy fullness. When He says to you, I know that thou hast got little strength; then say you to Him, I know that Thou hast got all strength – that Thou art all-mighty. When He says to you, I know thy folly; then say you to Him, I know Thy wisdom – what treasures of wisdom and knowledge are in Thee. When He says unto you, I know what darkness is in thee; then say you to Him, I know what light is in Thee. For what does David say in the 139th Psalm?

O LORD, Thou hast searched me, and known me. Thou knowest my downsitting and mine uprising; thou understandest my thought afar off. Thou compassest my path and my lying down, and art acquainted with all my ways. For there is not a word in my tongue, but, lo, O LORD, Thou knowest it altogether;

and then rejoicing he says:

How precious also are thy thoughts unto me, O God! How great is the sum of them! Search me, O God, and know my heart: try me, and know my thoughts: and see if there be any wicked way in me, and lead me in the way everlasting.

But then Jesus knows your good works too; He knows every cup of water given for His sake; He knows every throb of love in your bosom for Himself – every act of affection to His people, to the brethren. Every believer feels that his own works are nothing, and it is right that he should feel so; every believer looks upon them in this way, because he feels there is so much vileness in everything he does – such a mixture of motives. For instance, if you were to be kind to a stranger, you may have in doing so but one grain of love to Christ, and a hundred grains of other feelings; perhaps love of praise, or a desire to be thought well of. Now I will tell you what Christ does; He sprinkles the hundred grains with His own blood, He forgets them all, and treasures up the one grain of love to Himself, and says unto you, 'I know thy works, and thy labour, and thy patience.'

The second thing Christ says in their praise is, 'Thou canst not bear them which are evil.' This is a sure mark of a Christian; they cannot

10

bear them which are evil: they say, 'Depart from me, all ye workers of iniquity, for the Lord hath heard the voice of my weeping.' Now, if I were to look around at a Christian here and there, I would find that they feel this; but I would like to see more of it, a great deal more. 'Come out from among them, and be ye separate, saith the Lord;' for there can never be friendship between Christ and the world. Not that you must not walk on the same streets with them; but if ye have to live in Sodom, be like Lot, who vexed his righteous soul from day to day with their unlawful deeds; but be ye rather like Abraham, and dwell in the land of Hebron. You are quite a different people from the world; 'ye are a chosen generation, a royal priesthood, a peculiar people;' you have a different birth, ye are born from above; you have a different education, ye are taught of God; you are on a different journey, you are travelling towards Zion; you have different resting places from the world, you rest by the wells of salvation; you have a different deathbed, you say, 'O death, where is thy sting? O grave, where is thy victory?' and you have a different home.

Notice now the third thing Christ says of them: 'Thou hast tried them which say they are apostles, and are not, and hast found them liars.' It is said that in the latter days many shall rise up saying they are Christ; *that day is nearer than some of you think.* Now are there not many false apostles in our day? Are there not some who try to deceive and lead away many? Try them by 'the law and the testimony; if they speak not according to this word, it is because there is no light in them.' If you bid them believe what they say, on their own word, believe it not; try them by the Word. The Bereans were more noble, they searched to see whether or not these things were so; be ye noble, with their nobility.

Now, let us see the fourth thing Christ says in their praise: 'And hast borne, and hast patience, and for my name's sake hast laboured, and hast not fainted.' It is far easier to do than to suffer; it is far easier to be a Whitfield, to preach from land's end to land's end, than to lie on a bed of sickness. We have much to make us faint, to make us sigh and cry for the abominations that are done in the midst of us: and mostly all of you have sorrows; some of you have sorrows that you never breathed beyond your own bosom, even sorrows without a name; and some of you have sorrows that you tell from kindred to kindred breast – you have sorrows, because your children care for none of these things, or because those who are dear to you are on beds of sickness. But we must not faint or grow weary, we must bear. Resignation is a very sweet grace: it can only be cultivated here. The believer has two kinds of graces – he has purity and resignation; God has purity, but God can have no resignation, for He has all sovereignty, He is all-mighty. Yet resignation to God's will is a very sweet grace; it is a flower that grows on the earth – it will not bloom yonder. It is much easier to go about a whole lifetime preaching, to preach night and day, than to be patient under sickness. There are many saints who suffered much upon earth, now shining the brightest in glory; just because they glorified God more than others by their patient submission.

Let us see what Jesus blames them for. He says, 'Nevertheless I have somewhat against thee, because thou hast left thy first love.' *Somewhat* is not in the original – it should not be there at all. We would think by this, it is some little thing. It should be, I *have* against thee, or, I have *this* against thee, that thou hast left thy first love. Now, do you know what it is to have

13

been in an agony, when awakened by God – to have seen your corruptions? And do you remember what you felt when you saw an unveiled Christ – when you saw first a crucified Christ? Do you remember when your sins accused you, and when you said, *Behold, my Surety, who shall condemn*?

When a beloved friend was ill, and when his bosom heaved, and his eye flashed, do you remember what gladness filled your breast at the first signs of returning health; when the eye became clearer, and the breast beat more quietly? And do you remember, too, what you felt when lying in the darkness of the night, and saying, Would God it were morning; when the first streak of light burst in upon you, with what gladness it filled your breast? And do you remember when first you were introduced to Christ – when first you entered into the presence of God – when you were enabled to say, He *is mine*? You had often heard of Him before; but do you remember the time when first you could say, 'My Beloved is mine'? What a burning love you had then in your breast! – do you remember the leap of joy that came into your bosom? This was *first love*, this *was the love of espousals*; and this is what you have left. Do you not remember sacraments, when you had a greater glow of love in your bosom to Christ, in the anticipation of them, than you have of our approaching sacrament?

I do not know, but I believe (I speak of my own parish, for I know it best) that there is no word I could find in the Bible, that I could address to you, that would be more applicable to most of you than this, and this is what Jesus is saying unto you this night, 'I have this against thee, because thou hast left thy first love.' It is not a man that has this against you, it is not I who have this against you, it is *Christ*; it is He who suffered for your sake; it is He who was crucified, who died on the cross, who left His home for your sake; it is *Jesus* that has this against you; and He is saying unto you, Was I such a small object of love, that ye could only love me for one night, that ye could not watch with me one hour, that ye grew weary of loving me so soon?

And I think I may apply this to the unconverted here; for although you never had the first love, still there are many among you who were much more anxious than you are now. Is hell less dreadful than when you were first awakened? Is it not worth while that you should be awakened again? There are many among you who have fled out of Sodom, but who have never entered Zoar.

And now, let us see *what will be the punishment of those who have left their first love*. 'Remember therefore from whence thou art fallen, and repent, and do the first works; or else I will come unto thee quickly, and will remove thy candlestick out of his place, except thou repent.'

Christ says that you are to remember from whence you have fallen. You were once built upon the corner stone – Oh how you have fallen! You were once as a red-hot coal – Oh how cold you have got! You once had more zeal for the cause of Christ. Oh how you have fallen! And whilst you sit and think of this, you are to repent and do the first works. What! Must I be converted again? Yes, you must be converted again, or else Christ will come quickly. You see He is to lose no time about it; so I pray you repent quickly, or else Christ will remove thy candlestick. Oh! How dreadful are the punishments of Christ! He may take away your minister; and He may also take away the light of His word. You see how it was with Jonah; for the sake of one backsliding soul a whole sea was put in motion. So may God, for the sake of some backsliding soul, remove your candlestick out of its place. O Lord, give me suffering; give me sickness, give me poverty, give me anything, give me death itself; but do not remove Thy light from me, for then I shall get dark and lifeless!

And, lastly, let us see what is said in the seventh verse, 'To him that overcometh will I give to eat of the tree of life, which is in the midst of the paradise of God.' And so we are fighting, we are in a warfare, and I know there are some of you who are struggling, struggling hard, and you are overcoming. Well, then, you shall eat of the tree of life; you shall eat of Christ, who is in the midst of the paradise of God. May this prove a happy sacrament to many of you if we ever see it, if our candlestick be not removed before then! May it be a sacrament that shall be unto you the renewal of your first love!

EXPOSITION 2

The Church in Smyrna

And unto the angel of the church in Smyrna write; These things saith the First and the Last, which was dead, and is alive; I know thy works, and tribulation, and poverty, (but thou art rich) and I know the blasphemy of them which say they are Jews, and are not, but are the synagogue of Satan. Fear none of those things which thou shalt suffer: behold, the devil shall cast some of you into prison, that ye may be tried; and ye shall have tribulation ten days: be thou faithful unto death, and I will give thee a crown of life. He that hath an ear, let him hear what the Spirit saith unto the churches; he that overcometh shall not be hurt of the second death (Rev. 2:8-11).

The last time I had the pleasure of speaking to you, it was about the Church of Ephesus; that Christ blamed it for something. He had this against her, that she had left her first love; and

19

He bids her repent, and do the first works; if not, He will come quickly and remove the candlestick out of its place. Ephesus was once one of the most flourishing Churches of Asia; but Jesus *did* come quickly, and He removed the candlestick. It is now only a heap of ruins. When the traveller is there, he goes over ancient archways, and heaps of stones, and the yellow corn is seen growing where Ephesus once stood. There is a village near where it was; and Mr. Hartley, a traveller, tells us that he found only one Christian in the whole village. So may God do with us – He may take away our candlestick. We have many churches just now and flourishing congregations: but God may leave us a heap of ruins, with only one Christian to tell us that the candlestick hath been taken away. So it was with Ephesus; but it is very different with Smyrna.

Notice, Christ does not blame her for one thing. What! Were the Christians of Smyrna so holy, that even the eye of Christ did not see any fault? Well, we can get no comfort from that; for if Jesus were to send us a letter, it would be full of blame. But no! The Christians of Smyrna were just what Christians are now; but Christ washed them in His own blood, and clothed their naked souls in His righteousness;

and therefore He saw them all fair. This message to Smyrna reminds me of the Epistle to the Philippians; it is all kindness, all love. So is this message of Christ's to the Christians in Smyrna; it is all mercy, peace, gentleness, kindness, and love. Smyrna is still one of the most flourishing towns of Asia; it has 100,000 inhabitants, and it has several churches, and two stations, where are Protestant ministers, just like our own. God lighteth the lamp wheresoever He will.

But let us now see the *message* that was sent to Smyrna, and notice:

The character Christ takes to Himself here. He takes different characters in all the messages to the seven churches; and it is very beautiful to remark that He takes a character which suits the case of each of them. To the Church of Ephesus He says, 'I am He that holdeth the seven stars in my right hand, and who walketh in the midst of the seven golden candlesticks;' showing them that He could remove the candlestick when He pleased. And *here* He takes His encouraging character, 'These things said the First and the Last, which was dead and is alive.'

Notice, in the first chapter of the Revelation,

what John says, when Jesus was revealed to him at Patmos, when 'His head and His hairs were white like wool, as white as snow, and His eyes were as a flame of fire, and His feet like unto fine brass, as if they burned in a furnace' – John says, 'When I saw Him, I fell at His feet as dead;' and Jesus said unto him, 'Fear not' – just what He used to say upon the earth. You remember He said to His disciples on the Sea of Galilee, 'Be not afraid;' and here, when John fainted, Jesus encouraged him by saying the very same words, 'Fear not;' and when on earth He used to stretch out His right hand – so John says He did to him, 'He laid His right hand upon me, saying unto me, Fear not.'

And Jesus says here, 'These things saith the First and the Last.' He was the first at creation, and He will be the last at it; it is He that will gather everything together like a scroll; it is He who will make all things new; He says, 'I will create new heavens and a new earth.'

And He is the first and the last in Providence. From the time when a child is born into the world, Christ directs all the providences that happen even unto its dying day.

And He is the first in Grace; it was He who

carried on the plan of salvation; and He was the last at it; it was He who said, 'It is finished.' It is He who laid the foundation-stone of this church, and it is He who will put on the top-stone; and He is the first at a work of grace in the soul, and He is the last at it – He will be with you in your dying hour. It is this that gives us hope, 'Being confident of this very thing, that He which hath begun a good work in you, will perform it until the day of Jesus Christ.'

And again, Jesus says of Himself here, He was dead and is alive again. How encouraging is this character of Christ! Jesus *was* dead – He has not still to die, it is all over. It is this that gives peace to an awakened soul, to know that Jesus *was* dead. Well, then, Christians, you are quite safe; no wrath can come upon you, every drop of God's wrath hath fallen on *His* head. You have no more cause to fear it falling upon you than you would have to fear a storm of thunder and lightning, or an earthquake that happened more than eighteen hundred years ago. This gives great peace.

But there is another thing that gives peace – Christ was dead and *is alive again*; He has risen, and has been accepted, and is now at the right hand of God; and we have peace from this, because we know that we shall be as pleasing and acceptable in the sight of the Father as Christ is. Jesus says, 'Father, I will that they also, whom Thou hast given me, be with me where I am; that they may behold my glory, which Thou hast given me: for Thou lovedst me before the foundation of the world.'

Let us see *what Christ says of the Church*. They had three kinds of troubles: 'I know thy works, and tribulation, and poverty.' Afflictions very often go together. One trial seldom comes alone; perhaps sickness, or bereavements, and then poverty. But as putting the tree into the bitter waters made them sweet, so methinks it makes the bitter cup sweet – that there is so much sweetness in the cup, that none of the bitter will be felt, because Jesus says, *I* know it. It is *Christ* that knows; He measures all your suffering; He will not give you too much or too little. And again, Christ says, ' I know the blasphemy of them which say they are Jews, and are not, but are the synagogue of Satan.'

Another of the Christian's troubles, and the third one that Christ mentions here, is Satan the devil; this is the worst of them all. The Church of Smyrna was very much tried, but it was the purest of them all: when gold is put into the fire, all its dross is taken away – so it was with the Smyrna Christians. Many of its members were burnt at the stake. Their bishop, Polycarp, a very precious man, was cruelly put to death: and it is not that Satan is not as busy now, but he is sometimes a roaring lion, and sometimes an angel of light. It is true we have not persecutions at present, for the devil just now is flattering men; Christians are mixed with the world, the chaff with the wheat. Christ's people can hardly be distinguished from the world, yet the world hates them as much as ever; 'Marvel not though the world hate you.' But the devil *may* come out again like the roaring lion seeking his prey. *Our prisons may again be filled with Christians.*

But let us now see *the encouragements that Christ gives*. He says, 'I know thy works, and tribulation, and poverty; but thou art rich.' I had rather Christ would say that of me, than all the wise men in the world; I had rather that Jesus would say unto me, Thou art rich, than that all the world should say it. *They* are very apt to say of Christians, They are poor; but it is because they are blind. I have no doubt this word in the Bible is very little believed, but it is no less true – 'Hath not God chosen the poor of this world, rich in faith, and heirs of the kingdom?' But do not mistake me, you will never get to heaven because you are poor; there are very few of the poor in my parish who seem to be rich in faith; and oh! If you are not in Christ, you are miserably poor, and will be miserably poorer still; but be ye rich in faith, and ye shall be heirs of the kingdom. Again Christ says, 'Fear none of those things which thou shalt suffer.' Oh, that is a sweet word – fear *none* of them, the smallest or the greatest of them. If you stand on the seashore, you will notice that sometimes after a very small wave, a very large one comes; so it is often with affliction; Christ sends a small trial first, that He may prepare you for a large one; but fear *none* of them. If you were to bear the burdens yourself, you would be overwhelmed; but take them to Jesus, lay them all upon Him, and then you will slip from under them, and you will have to bear nothing. I believe there is not one who is a Christian here, but who will have to suffer in some way or other; for it is written, Thou *shalt* suffer. But fear *none* of them; fear not tribulation and poverty, fear not reproaches, fear not persecution, fear *none* of these things which thou *shalt* suffer.

And here is another of Christ's encouragements: 'Be thou faithful unto death, and I will give thee a crown of life.' 'He that overcometh shall not be hurt of the second death.' The second death! And are there two deaths? Yes. Have you ever been at a death-bed? Have you ever seen the eyes roll back, the lips quiver, and the hands grow cold and motionless? Have you ever seen the death-bed of an awakened sinner, of one who cried out, Oh for another day! Oh for another hour! Oh for another moment! – of one who was *obliged* to die? Well then, that is but a shadow of the second death.

When you are walking on the road, and when the sun causes you to see your figure, that is only the shadow – the substance is the real thing; so it is agreed by the soundest divines (and I believe it is true) that God intended the first death to be a type, or shadow, of the second death of the Christless soul; and if the first, the shadow, be so dreadful, what will the second death be? – when it shall be eternally dying, but never dead; when you shall be wishing to die, but are not able! When you see one ill with fever, he is anxious to get water, but he cannot swallow it; and this is but a type of the burning thirst of those who have died without Christ, when they shall ask for a drop of water to cool their parched tongue.

But it is very different with the believer;

death is no death to him, for Christ hath taken away its sting; it is to him an entrance into life; and then he shall not be hurt of the second death – it shall pass by, but shall not touch him.

And again, Jesus says, 'Be thou faithful unto death, and I will give thee a crown of life.' It is called in one place a crown of gold, in another a crown of righteousness, in another a crown of glory, and here it is said to be a crown of life – it shall never fade! But what is meant by being faithful unto death? It is to be believing unto the end, to believe unto your dying hour; and then, when God wipes away the tears, Christ shall put on the crown.

EXPOSITION 3

The Church in Pergamos

And to the angel of the church in Pergamos write; These things saith He which hath the sharp sword with two edges; I know thy works, and where thou dwellest, even where Satan's seat is: and thou holdest fast my name, and hast not denied my faith, even in those days wherein Antipas was my faithful martyr, who was slain among you, where Satan dwelleth. But I have a few things against thee, because thou hast there them that hold the doctrine of Balaam, who taught Balac to cast a stumbling-block before the children of Israel, to eat things sacrificed unto idols, and to commit fornication. So hast thou also them that hold the doctrine of the Nicolaitans, which thing I hate. Repent; or else I will come unto thee quickly, and will fight against them with the sword of my mouth. He that hath an ear, let him hear what the Spirit saith unto the churches; To him that overcometh will I give to eat of the hidden manna, and will

give him a white stone, and in the stone a
new name written, which no man knoweth
saving he that receiveth it (Rev. 2:12-17).

We spoke of Ephesus; Christ had this against
her, that she had left her first love, and He took
away her candlestick, and now there is not one
Christian in Ephesus. We spoke of Smyrna, in
which even the eye of Christ saw nothing to
blame; and now we come to Pergamos, in
which He saw something to approve, and
something also to blame. Jesus says of it, it is
where Satan's seat is – or, it should be, where
Satan's throne is.

Pergamos was the capital of one of the
provinces of Asia Minor; it was a very
flourishing town; there was a great deal of
riches there, it was there that the king lived,
and it was the seat of much learning. There
was a library in it containing two hundred
thousand books. It was at Pergamos that
parchment first was made, and hence it got its
name. It was the seat of riches, of royalty, and
of learning, and yet it was where Satan's throne
was; and so it is very often, wherever there are
riches, or much human wisdom, it is there that
the devil holds his court. Jesus said of Smyrna,
'I know thy works, and tribulation, and poverty,

but thou art rich;' but it was very different with Pergamos. Christ removed the candlestick from Ephesus, but He did not do that with Pergamos: He said, if it did not repent, He would come and fight against it; and so Pergamos is standing to this day. The last traveller that was there in 1820 tells us that there are in it fifteen thousand inhabitants, and the tenth of these are nominally Christians, who have two churches; so the lamp is yet burning there, although but dimly.

But let us see now *the character that Christ takes to Himself here*. He takes one always suited to the Church to which He writes. He says, 'These things saith He that hath the sharp sword with two edges.' Old divines say that this two-edged sword is grace; because they say that grace cannot come out of any mouth but out of Christ's; and they take this passage, 'Thou art fairer than the children of men, grace is poured into Thy lips;' and this, in the Song of Solomon, 'His mouth is most sweet, yea, He is altogether lovely.' And the sword has two edges; the one edge convinces of sin, the other gives peace; the one rends the veil that hides your sins from you, the other edge rends the veil that hides Christ from you, and reveals

Him unto you; the one edge wounds the soul, the other shows the Physician, and lets the healing balm flow over the wounded soul.

Those of you who like the way that the old divines explain it may keep it. But now this sword is thought to be the sword of judgment. Read with me in the nineteenth chapter of Revelation, the eleventh verse:

> And I saw heaven opened, and behold a white horse; and He that sat upon him was called Faithful and True; and in righteousness He doth judge and make war. His eyes were as a flame of fire, and on His head were many crowns; and He had a name written, that no man knew, but He Himself; and He was clothed with a vesture dipped in blood: and His name is called the Word of God. And the armies which were in heaven followed Him upon white horses, clothed in fine linen, white and clean. And out of His mouth goeth a sharp sword, that with it He should smite the nations: and He shall rule them with a rod of iron: and He treadeth the wine-press of the fierceness and wrath of Almighty God. And He hath on His vesture and on His thigh a name written, KING OF KINGS AND LORD OF LORDS.

It says here, that He out of whose mouth cometh the sword shall smite the nations; and in the fourth of Hebrews, at the eleventh verse, it is written:

> Let us labour therefore to enter into that rest, lest any man fall after the same example of unbelief. For the word of God is quick, and powerful, and sharper than any two-edged sword, piercing even to the dividing asunder of soul and spirit, and of the joints and marrow, and is a discerner of the thoughts and intents of the heart.

What I notice from this is, that Christ has two characters; He is a Saviour, and also a Destroyer; He is all Saviour *now*, but He will *one day* smite the nations. What I wish is, that you would now be convinced with that sword, and brought to peace by it, and you would not fall under it *then*.

Let us now see *the charge that Christ gives to the Church of Pergamos*. First, Their danger: 'I know thy works, and where thou dwellest, even where Satan's seat is.' This is very comforting, that a believer cannot go to any place but Jesus knows it. Do you live in an ungodly family, a lily among many thorns? Christ says to you, I know where thou dwellest. Do you live in an ungodly neighbourhood?

Christ says to you, I know where thou dwellest, even where Satan's seat is. The devil had his throne at Pergamos, and is he not in this town too? He holds his court here; he has many ambassadors; he sways his sceptre here. Why do so many sit hardened under the word, but by the power of the devil? Why do so many keep away from the house of God altogether, but by his power? It has been often noticed, that in many places, for the sake of Christians who have gone before, God still preserves a seed. So it is with Pergamos; there were some faithful Christians there, and there are some Christians there yet; and this is perhaps the reason that God is preserving a few believers here for there were once faithful Christian men in this place – the lamp is still burning here, although but dimly.

Let us see *what Christ says in their praise*. 'And thou holdest fast my name' – hold fast by Jesus; and again, 'hast not denied my faith.' This is the grand secret, to hold fast Jesus' name, and then you will not deny His faith; there is nothing can give boldness like that. To keep close to Christ in secret, having near communion with God; there is nothing can give boldness like that. It is said the righteous are bold as a lion; keep close then to Christ, hold Him fast, or rather He will hold you.

> Even in those days wherein Antipas was my faithful martyr, who was slain among you, where Satan dwelleth.

Who is this Antipas – who ever heard of him – who is he? There is no other book mentions his name – we have quite forgotten him, but Christ remembers his name; it is written on His heart. 'My faithful martyr Antipas!'

Perhaps there are some believers among you who are very poor – who were never half a mile from home – who, when you go out, do not see twelve persons that you think would shed a tear over your grave; but Jesus knows you – He has written you upon His heart. I often wonder that we so soon forget each other. In our little company of Christians, some have been taken away; and although we think of them sometimes, yet when we remember their bright countenances, and the way that they looked up listening to the word, they were very dear Christians; and yet how little we remember them! How soon have we forgotten them! But Christ does not forget them – He remembers them. That is what is meant when it is said, 'The righteous shall be had in everlasting remembrance;' they are written upon His heart, and Jesus knows their name – 'My faithful martyr Antipas!'

But Christ had also something in them to blame.

But I have a few things against thee, because thou hast there them that hold the doctrine of Balaam, who taught Balak to cast a stumbling-block before the children of Israel, to eat things sacrificed unto idols, and to commit fornication.

Balaam dared not curse Israel, when God had blessed; but he caused Balak to put a stumbling-block before them. And are there not some of us, are there not some of *you*, who have respect for ordinances, for the preached word, for the bread and wine, who dare not *openly* oppose Christians, but who put a stumbling-block in their way?

So hast thou them also that hold the doctrine of the Nicolaitans, which thing I hate.

And are there any of you who have in your house those who are not Christians? Parents, you may be Christians yourselves; but if you speak only to your children, you are like old Eli, who spoke to his children, but who did not restrain them. Are there some of you, who have for your companions those who hold the doctrine of the Nicolaitans? Take care, this was the sin of Pergamos. Say you unto them, 'Depart from me, for God hath heard the voice of my weeping.' And what is the judgment that Christ threatens? – He says, Repent, or else ' I will come unto thee quickly, and will fight against them with the sword of my mouth.'

Last, *what is the reward to them that overcome*! 'I will give him to eat of the hidden manna.' You will find this explained in the sixteenth chapter of Exodus:

> And the house of Israel called the name thereof Manna: and it was like coriander seed, white; and the taste of it was like wafers made with honey. And Moses said, This is the thing which the LORD commandeth, Fill an omer of it, to be kept for your generations; that they may see the bread wherewith I have fed you in the wilderness, when I brought you forth from the land of Egypt. And Moses said unto Aaron, Take a pot, and put an omer full of manna therein, and lay it up before the LORD, to be kept for your generations. As the LORD commanded Moses, so Aaron laid it up before the Testimony, to be kept.

And so Christ is the hidden manna; He is hidden from us *just now*, but we shall yet eat of the hidden manna, we shall feed upon Christ. He says, I will give you myself. And what could He give us more?

And again, 'I will give him a white stone, and in the stone a new name written, which no man knoweth saving he that receiveth it.' At the Grecian games, those who won the race got a white stone, and there was a name written on it, which no man knew but the person who got it: and so, if *we* overcome, we will get a white stone; but we get it *even here*, for who can tell the peace that a believer feels? Others know nothing of it; no man can know but those whose sins are forgiven, what it is to feel the peace of forgiveness of sins. The world thinks that we are sour-tempered when we will not join with them – when we look solemn; but they do not know the peace that is within. Oh, then, dear anxious souls, come to Christ, and you will have this peace, too.

But believers will *yet* get a white stone. Oh! Who can tell the peace that we shall have when Christ shall put a crown on our head? Oh! who can tell the joy that will burn in our bosom, when we feel that our hearts are quite clean, when we see that we are dressed in a white robe, in linen clean and white, which is the righteousness of saints? – and no one will know that peace, except he who has it. Those who are standing on the left side of the judge will know nothing of it. We are in a warfare just now, but is it not a race worth running? Let us overcome, and we will eat of the hidden manna, and we will get a white stone, and in the stone a new name written, which no man knoweth saving he that receiveth it.

EXPOSITION 4

The Church in Thyatira

And unto the angel of the church in Thyatira write; These things saith the Son of God, who hath His eyes like unto a flame of fire, and His feet are like fine brass; I know thy works, and charity, and service, and faith, and thy patience, and thy works; and the last to be more than the first. Notwithstanding I have a few things against thee, because thou sufferest that woman Jezebel, which calleth herself a prophetess, to teach and to seduce my servants to commit fornication, and to eat things sacrificed unto idols. And I gave her space to repent of her fornication; and she repented not. Behold, I will cast her into a bed, and them that commit adultery with her into great tribulation, except they repent of their deeds. And I will kill her children with death; and all the churches shall know that I am He which searcheth the reins and hearts: and I will give unto every one of you according to your works. But unto you

I say, and unto the rest in Thyatira (as many as have not this doctrine, and which have not known the depths of Satan, as they speak), I will put upon you none other burden. But that which ye have already hold fast till I come. And he that overcometh, and keepeth my works unto the end, to him will I give power over the nations: and he shall rule them with a rod of iron; as the vessels of a potter shall they be broken to shivers: even as I received of my Father. And I will give him the morning star. He that hath an ear, let him hear what the Spirit saith unto the churches (Rev. 2:18-29).

Thyatira is only once again mentioned in the Bible, and it is very sweetly mentioned; it is where the account is given of the conversion of Lydia, and of the jailor. It says, 'Lydia was of the city of Thyatira.' When Paul preached at Philippi, these were perhaps the two most unlikely persons in the place; and yet *these were the very two* who were to be brought to Christ. Lydia was a stranger in the town of Philippi; perhaps, if she had remained at Thyatira, she might have been seduced by that woman Jezebel; but God brought her here. God always converts in His own way; He fixes upon strangers; He has the threads of every soul in His hand, and He draws the soul, and brings it to the *very spot* where the Sun of Righteousness is to rise upon it. Has God done this with some of you? Has He not taken some of you who were strangers? God sometimes converts a soul in the bosom of its own family, and sometimes in a strange land; and *it is always a sweet place to that soul where it first saw Christ*.

Ephesus had left her first love; Smyrna was poor and yet rich; Pergamos was where Satan's throne was; and now we come to Thyatira. All that we know about it is from books; there is no history given of it in the Bible. Very little is known about it, except by Christ; He knows the history of every place, and His history *is always the truest*. There are five thousand inhabitants in Thyatira; the houses are mostly made of mud; the town was taken by the Turks, and remains at this time in their possession. It is no longer Thyatira, but called by a Turkish name; but there are yet a few Christians there. The last missionary who was there, Mr. Parsons, says: There is yet a form of godliness; there are two churches, and two schools, and there are a few Greek and Armenian Christians who meet on the Sabbath-day.

The character Christ takes to Himself here. 'These things saith the Son of God.' Those of you who are believers, this *is just what gives you peace, to know that Jesus is divine*, to know that He is the Son of God; because then you know that He has got all strength and all might. 'His name shall be called Wonderful, Counsellor, the Mighty God, the Everlasting Father, the Prince of Peace.' Cling to your *Divine Saviour*. But then this is a word of awful power to the unconverted, that He is the Son of God; that He is an infinite, an immoveable, a divine, an eternal rock.

And then Christ's 'eyes are like unto a flame of fire.' If you put wood into the fire, it soon pierces through it; if you put stone in, it even pierces through it; or if you put iron in, it pierces through it too – nothing can withstand fire. So it is with the eyes of Christ; they pierce and penetrate through everything.

I told you this *before* the Lord's Supper, to try and keep away those of you who are without Christ; and now God has brought me to you, to tell it you again *after* the Lord's Supper, for a different reason. I would say to those of you who know you are Christless, 'Remember man looketh only on the outward appearance, but Christ looketh on the heart: He not only looks on the heart, but He looks *into* the heart: He *searches*, He *looks through*, He knows all your wishes and designs.' He says in the twenty-third verse of this chapter, 'I am He which searcheth the reins and hearts.' And there are some of you who were cleaving to Christ, but who seem already to have mixed with the world. Christ's eye sees you; He has got eyes like unto a flame of fire; He has *followed* you.

Those of you who are Christians, I would like you to look more at a *whole Christ*; not to take only part of Christ. You like to think of His eyes as they were on earth; you like to think of Him when He wept over Jerusalem, when He stood by the widow of Nain, when He was at the grave of Lazarus; for it is written, 'Jesus wept.' And God forbid that I should make you think less of the compassion of Christ; for it is great. No one can know the compassion that He has, the *infinite* compassion that is in Him; especially for those of you who do not love Him, His eyes are as it were streaming down with tears. But I would like Christians to remember, too, that Christ's eyes are like a flame of fire.

And again, Christ's 'feet are like fine brass'. In the first chapter it is said, 'as if they burned in a furnace.' Now what are they like brass for?

– that they may trample. You like to think of Christ as Isaiah did, when he says, 'How beautiful upon the mountains are the feet of Him that bringeth good tidings, that publisheth peace; that bringeth good tidings of good, that publisheth salvation; that saith unto Zion, Thy God reigneth!' As the two Marys did, when they clasped His feet; and as the woman did which had been a sinner; but the feet of Christ are also like fine brass, to tread down His enemies.

In Micah 4:13, it is written, 'Arise and thresh, O daughter of Zion; for I will make thine horn iron, and I will make thy hoofs brass: and thou shalt beat in pieces many people: and I will consecrate their gain unto the LORD, and their substance unto the Lord of the whole earth.' They used to put brass hoofs on the cattle, and send them into the thrashing-floors to thrash the corn; and Christ seems to allude to that here.

And in the sixty-third of Isaiah it is written: 'Who is this that cometh from Edom, with dyed garments from Bozrah? this that is glorious in His apparel, travelling in the greatness of His strength? I that speak in righteousness, mighty to save.'

And in the nineteenth of Revelation it is said

that, when John saw Christ, 'His eyes were as a flame of fire, and on His head were many crowns; and He had a name written, that no man knew but He Himself: And He was clothed with a vesture dipped in blood: and His name is called the Word of God.'

Now, what shall we learn from all this? That Christ is not only a Saviour, but an Avenger too. He is the shadow of a great rock, where any weary soul may find refuge; and to those who have no covering, He says, 'I counsel you to buy of me white raiment that thou mayest be clothed, and that the shame of thy nakedness do not appear.' But He is an *Avenger* too – He will trample, He will tread down the *Christless*, and their blood will stain all His raiment. How much better to take Christ, as coming with His feet beautiful upon the mountains, than with His feet of brass as an avenger!

Let us now see *what is the character Christ gives to Thyatira*. The people in Thyatira put me in mind of Jeremiah's figs: the good among them were very good, and the bad were very bad. Let us look first at the good parts. Jesus says, 'I know thy works,' – we have spoken of that before; and 'charity': throughout all the Bible, *this word* means *love*; and it should

47

rather be thus rendered. It is said of the woman who was a sinner, she was forgiven much, therefore she loved much. Do you love much? The fruit of the Spirit is love – faith worketh by love. Among all the graces that are spoken of in the fifth chapter of Galatians, love is first mentioned. The buds of the trees, as the leaves open out in spring, are of a beautiful light-green colour; so love is the first budding of the branch that is joined to the vine – the first budding of the soul that is united to Christ. Can you say, 'Lord, Thou knowest all things, Thou knowest that I love Thee!' Do you love Christ? Do you love the Christians? 'By this shall all men know that ye are my disciples, if ye have love one to another.' 'Little children, love one another.' I know thy charity and 'service'. Christians are helpful to one another. When Jesus washed His disciples' feet, He said, 'If I then, your Lord and Master, have washed your feet, ye also ought to wash one another's feet. For I have given you an example, that you should do as I have done to you.' Do you know the meaning of this? I believe there are some of you who, although you were to think for a hundred years, would not find it out: if you had love, then you would know the meaning of ' So ought ye also to wash one another's feet.' 'If any man will do the will of God, he shall know of the doctrine whether it be of God.'

And again, I know thy 'service and faith'. It is strange that Christ should mention love and service before faith. It is just because the more love and service you have, the more faith you will have. When a tree grows taller, its roots grow farther down; it takes deeper and deeper hold of the earth: so the more love you have, the more you do: you will have the more faith – it will take deeper root. And thy 'patience'; when a sailor is clinging to a rock – when the waves come one after another, and try to suck him away – he perseveres the more, he holds the faster to the rock. Why? Because it is for his life. So, when Christians have escaped out of the black waves of this world – when they are holding by the rock – the waves come and try to suck them away, and sink them in the whirlpool. What does this make you do? It makes you persevere the more – it makes you hold the faster to your Rock – cling the closer to Christ – endure to the end. Why? Because it is for your life.

'And thy works; and the last to be more than the first.' Are *our* last works more than the first? Are we doing more after this sacrament than after last sacrament? But there *are* some of you, I know, whose last works *are* more than the first. Ephesus had left her first love, and Christ bid her repent quickly, and do the first works: *how much more blessed* to have the Saviour say unto you, that thy last works are more than the first! – 'He died for us, that we who live, should not henceforth live unto ourselves, but unto Him who died for us, and who rose again.'

Let us now see *what Christ had to blame*. It is written, 'I suffer not a woman to teach, nor to usurp authority over the man, but to be in silence.'

All the men of God have come to the conclusion, that a woman should not speak; and if you will only go to the Bible, and read it as little children without being prejudiced, you will see that a woman should not teach, but should learn at home. This Jezebel was a wicked woman: 'Notwithstanding I have a few things against thee because thou sufferest that woman Jezebel, which calleth herself a prophetess, to teach and to seduce my servants to commit fornication, and to eat things sacrificed unto idols.'

Now, what should they have done? They should have opposed her. Are there no Jezebels

among ourselves, who try to seduce Christ's
servants? I will mention a circumstance which
has happened in this place, and I do it for the
sake of the children of God who have been
seduced. We lately sat down at the Lord's
Supper; and would the Devil let us alone? Oh
no! There was what is called an Oratorio in
the Popish Chapel; I wish you did not know
what it means. It is taking passages out of the
Word of God, and setting them to music, and
they are sung by profane persons: they take
the sweetest words in the Bible; the very *words
that are life to a believer*. Was this not one of
the depths of Satan? Now we should have set
our face against it. You sat down and took the
cup of the Lord, and then went and took the
cup of devils; you were sitting in the *temple of
the Lord*, and will you go and sit in the temple
of idols?[1]

---

[1]Mr. M'Cheyne then read the following extract
from the Rev. John Newton:

'Whereunto shall we liken the people of this
generation, and to what are they like? I represent
to myself a number of persons of various
characters, involved in one common charge of high
treason. They are already in a state of confinement,
but not yet brought to their trial. The facts, however,
are so plain, and the evidence against them so

'And I gave her space to repent.' See the long-suffering of Christ. *You* have got space, too, to repent. But what is the judgment of Christ – what will He do? 'I will kill her children with death.' How dreadful! – with death!

---

strong and pointed, that there is not the least doubt of their guilt being fully proved, and that nothing but a pardon can preserve them from punishment. In this situation it should seem their wisdom to avail themselves of every expedient in their power for obtaining mercy. But they are entirely regardless of their danger, and wholly taken up with contriving methods of amusing themselves, that they may pass away the term of their imprisonment with as much cheerfulness as possible. Among other resources they call in the assistance of music; and amidst a great variety of subjects in this way, they are particularly pleased with one. They choose to make the solemnities of their impending trial, the character of their judge, the methods of his procedure, and the awful sentence to which they are exposed, the groundwork of a musical entertainment; and, as if they were quite unconcerned in the event, their attention is chiefly fixed upon the skill of the composer, in adapting the style of his music to the very solemn language and subject with which they are trifling. The king, however, out of his great clemency and compassion

But now what is the message? 'He that overcometh, and keepeth my works unto the end.' Let us fight, let us go forward as Christians, not fearing any man; and it is not enough that you keep Christ's *words* to the end, you must keep His *works* too, to the very end. 'And I will give him power over the nations: and he shall rule them with a rod of iron; as the vessels of a potter shall they be broken to

---

towards those who have no pity for themselves, presents them with his goodness. Undesired by them, he sends them a gracious message. He assures them that he is unwilling they should suffer: he requires, yea, he entreats them to submit. He points out a way in which their confession and submission shall be certainly accepted; and in this way, which he condescends to prescribe, he offers them a free and a full pardon. But instead of taking a single step towards a compliance with his goodness, they set his message likewise to music, and this together with a description of their present state, and of the fearful doom awaiting them if they continue obstinate, is sung for their diversion, accompanied with the sound of cornet, flute, harp, sackbut, psaltery, dulcimer, and all kinds of instruments, Dan. iii. 5. Surely if such a case as I have supposed could be found in real life, though I might admire the musical taste of those people, I should commiserate their insensibility.'

shivers: even as I received of my Father.' I do not know what this means; Christ says, I will put you upon a throne; and again He says, Dost thou not know that thou shalt judge angels? And here He says, He will give us power over the nations. I do not know what this is, but it will be a great glory.

And lastly, the reward: 'I will give him the morning star.' Now, what is this star? It is Christ – 'I am the bright and morning star.' Balaam says, 'There shall come a star out of Jacob, and a sceptre shall rise out of Israel.' When we see the morning star in the east we say it will soon be daybreak. So, when we see the morning star going to rise upon any soul, we say of that soul, It will soon be daybreak, the day will soon dawn. But Christ says He will *give* us the morning star, which is Himself; He says He will give us to eat of the tree of life, which is Himself; He says He will give us to eat of the hidden manna, which is hidden Christ; and here He says He will give us the 'morning star.' He is our own Saviour even *now*, and will be our own Saviour then, when we stand with Him in glory on the confines of the other world; when we are where there will be no night, where it will be all day; Jesus will give us the morning star.

EXPOSITION 5

The Church in Sardis

And unto the angel of the church in Sardis write; These things saith He that hath the seven Spirits of God, and the seven stars; I know thy works, that thou hast a name that thou livest, and art dead. Be watchful, and strengthen the things which remain, that are ready to die: for I have not found thy works perfect before God. Remember therefore how thou hast received and heard, and hold fast, and repent. If therefore thou shalt not watch, I will come on thee as a thief, and thou shalt not know what hour I will come upon thee. Thou hast a few names even in Sardis which have not defiled their garments; and they shall walk with me in white: for they are worthy. He that overcometh, the same shall be clothed in white raiment; and I will not blot out his name out of the book of life, but I will confess his name before my Father, and before His angels. He that hath an ear, let him hear what the Spirit saith unto the churches (Rev. 3:1-6).

We now come to Sardis. Of all the churches, I think this applies best to us. It is wonderful how there is something in every one of them that suits ourselves, as if Christ had written *our* name instead of theirs; but the message to Sardis seems to apply to us more than any of them, for we have a name to live, and we are dead.

The character Christ takes to Himself here. First, 'These things saith He that hath the seven Spirits of God.' How does He get the name of the seven Spirits of God? If you will look to the first chapter of the Revelation, you will find it explained,

> John to the seven churches which are in Asia: Grace be unto you, and peace, from Him which is, and which was, and which is to come; and from the seven Spirits which are before His throne; and from Jesus Christ, who is the faithful Witness, and the first-begotten of the dead, and the Prince of the kings of the earth.

There is a blessing here from the *whole* of the Godhead. Christ has got the seven Spirits of God. Seven is often used in the Bible; and in the Hebrew it means *full*. So Christ has the full Spirit of God – He had the Spirit for

Himself, God gave it to Him without measure; Jesus had it not as His brethren, or His fellows; for 'Thou hast anointed Him with the oil of gladness above His fellows.'

And some of you will remember where it is said, 'I the Lord hath called Thee in righteousness, and I will hold Thine hand, and will keep Thee, and give Thee for a covenant of the people, for a light of the Gentiles.' Though it was Christ that was to lay down His life, yet He needed God to hold Him up; and, as if He would shrink back from it, God encourages Him, just like a child who, having to go through a deep water, would say, 'Father, I dare not go through;' and his father would answer, 'Do not be afraid, my child, I will hold your hand;' so God said to His Son, I will hold Thine hand, and will keep Thee.

And Christ says in Isaiah, 'The Spirit of the Lord God is upon me: because the Lord hath anointed me to preach good tidings unto the meek; He hath sent me to bind up the broken-hearted, to proclaim liberty to the captives, and the opening of the prison to them that are bound,' etc. The *Father* ministered unto Him, the *Spirit* ministered unto Him, and *angels* ministered unto Him. Christ had not only the Spirit for *Himself*, but for *us*, too; so that we may come and take of His fullness, even grace for grace. 'I will pray the Father, and He shall give you another Comforter, that He may abide with you forever: even the Spirit of Truth.' 'Be not drunk with wine, wherein is excess; but be filled with the Spirit.' There is an *infinite* fullness in Christ; so that we may come and drink *continually* at that fountain; and remember what is written, 'If ye, then, being evil, know how to give good gifts unto your children; how much more shall your heavenly Father give the Holy Spirit to them that ask Him!'

Second, *He holdeth 'the seven stars'*. Christ took the same character in His address to Ephesus, and we saw that the stars are His ministers. First, Christ has the stars in His right hand, *in order that He may give them*. We are wanting ministers to this place, and I believe in my heart that it is God that has stirred us up to it. Now if you would look to Christ to give the stars, there would be less planning, less scheming among men, and I may say, among *yourselves*. Look *more* to the hand of Christ; look less to man: let us pray that Christ will give us stars, out of His own right hand. And, second, *Christ lets them shine*. When you have got your minister, you perhaps, after coming out of church, say, 'I was quite disappointed with that man, I really heard nothing today:' and that is perhaps all true; but then ministers only shine, in so far as Christ opens His hand to let them shine. Our sky is very dark just now; and if we are to look for stars to shine brighter, we must look to the hand of Christ. And, third, *He will take them away*. It is *Christ* who puts the stars in any place, and it is *Christ* who takes them away, and puts them in another place, or takes them out of the sky altogether. Christ took away the candlestick from Ephesus; and if you do not become a godly people, I believe in my heart that Christ will take the stars away. Use the light while you have it: 'Be ye doers of the word, and not hearers only, deceiving your own selves.' You have the light just now, you may not have it another month; *follow ministers*, in as far as they follow Christ – follow them in so far as they lead you to Christ – follow them in so far as they are the star of Bethlehem, to lead you to the place where the young child lies.

Let us see what Christ has to blame in Sardis. He says, 'I know thy works, that thou hast a name that thou livest, and art dead.' All the people in Sardis may have gone to church, and although there are thousands in this place who have not even the name to live, who never enter the house of God, still there are many of you who come to church, who attend the prayer meeting, and you have a name to live, and yet you are dead. Where is the Christian who has living faith? Where is the Christian who has living love burning in his bosom to God? Where is the Christian who has living service, kind and affectionate, to the brethren? Oh how different from Brainerd's Indians! You should be ready to distribute, willing to communicate. Where will we find a Dorcas, full of good works and alms-deeds? Where shall we find those who, when bereaved of their children are still and know that it is God? Where are those who, when afflicted, say, 'It is well'?

The sweet counsel of Christ. 'Be watchful, and strengthen the things which remain, that are ready to die: for I have not found thy works perfect before God.' There were some that remained in Sardis; and so there are some *here* who are ready to die; there are some of you who seemed a little pricked on the Sabbath, or at the prayer meeting, and perhaps you awoke in the same state in the morning; but it just went off during the day. You are like a broken flower, or a sickly child, ready to die. Now 'strengthen the things which remain.' 'O Ephraim, what shall I do unto thee? O Judah, what shall I do unto thee? For your goodness is as a morning cloud, and as the early dew it goeth away.' You are like those who receive the Word gladly, and have no root in themselves, and so endure but for a time; for afterwards, when affliction or persecution ariseth for the Word's sake, immediately they are offended.

Second direction, 'Be watchful.' The devil is watchful, the world is watchful, and why should not *you* be watchful? Take heaven by violence; 'Strive to enter in at the strait gate.' If you were walking with a candle on a stormy night, would you not hold your hands all round it, that no wind might get in to blow it out? And so you should do with the candle that is almost out in your breast; you should watch, you should not go into the world, lest any gust of wind come and blow it out. You are like a bruised reed, or the smoking flax; and God will not break the bruised reed, nor quench the smoking flax; see that *you* do not do it. Remember Lot's wife; she went a little way, but she looked back. Remember how you once felt, how you once received and heard the word, and forget not Christ's word, 'Hold fast and repent.'

The punishment:– 'If therefore thou shalt not watch, I will come on thee as a thief, and thou shalt not know what hour I will come upon thee.' In Smyrna, in Pergamos, and in Thyatira, there are yet Christians; but in Ephesus and in Sardis there are none. In the year of our Lord 400, Sardis was taken by the Goths; and it is now called by the name of Sarte. Mr. Pliny Fisk, the last missionary that was there, 1820, says that it is a miserable place, the people are mostly all herdsmen, and the houses are made of mud. It was on a Sabbath when they were there, and he says, 'We read to them the address to the church in Sardis, and then the account of the Day of Judgment (Matt. 25). We could not refrain from weeping while we sang the seventy-fourth Psalm, and prayed among the ruins of Sardis.' Once there were there those who praised the Lord, and now there is not one Christian in the miserable village of Sarte. So you see Christ did come, and take away the star from Sardis; and if you repent not, He may do the same with you; and there may come a day when travellers shall pass by *here*, and weep, when they think that in this place

Christians once met to praise the Lord. 'Jesus Christ is the same yesterday, and today, and for ever.'

Let us *now turn to the few who were in Sardis*. 'Thou hast a few names even in Sardis which have not defiled their garments.' We are only a few; but yet we shall make a company which no man can number. Christians are always as a lily among many thorns. Observe Jesus never omits one Christian – the Lord knoweth Antipas! And there are some here, who walk through the streets, but who do not defile their garments. We are helpers of your joy, and you are our joy and crown of rejoicing.

Let us *now see the promise to them that overcome*.

1. 'They shall walk with me in white, for they are worthy.'

2. 'The same shall be clothed in white raiment.'

3. 'And I will not blot out his name out of the book of life.'

4. 'But I will confess His name before my Father, and before His angels.'

It is the same raiment that we have here, the same white raiment that we shall be clothed in yonder. All other blood washes red, *this* blood washes white as snow. And we shall walk with Christ; we shall walk with Him as *companions*; 'Henceforth I call you not servants, but friends.' We shall walk with Him as *children*; He shall say, 'Behold, I, and the children that Thou hast given me.' We shall walk with Him as *brethren*; He is our Elder Brother. We shall walk with Him as our *husband*. 'Who is this that cometh up from the wilderness, leaning upon her Beloved?' His left hand is under my head; we shall follow the Lamb whithersoever He goeth.

There was a little Christian child who was asked, when she was dying, why she was so happy? 'Because,' she said, 'I am going to be with Christ.' 'But,' they said to her, 'perhaps Christ will leave heaven.' 'Ah! Then,' she said, 'I will leave it, too, and go with Him.' It is our very heaven to be with Christ; we shall see eye to eye.

'I am in a strait betwixt two, having a desire to depart and to be with Christ, which is far better.'

'To her was granted that she should be arrayed in fine linen, clean and white: for the fine linen is the righteousness of saints.'

'Rejoice not that the spirits are subject unto

you, but rather rejoice because your names are written in heaven.'

There are some who sat with us here, who are now walking with Christ in white. Does Christ ever blot any name out of the book of life? Yes. But those of us who overcome shall not be blotted out of the book of life; but He will confess our name before His Father, and before His angels. There are some of you who are contented if you be looked upon as religious, and, as Christ says unto you, you have your reward. And there are others of you who have to bear reproaches; and when you fall into sin, some of those who look upon you will never allow that you are Christians; but *Christ* knows you, and all those that overcome He will confess before His Father, and before His angels. May this be the lot of many!

EXPOSITION 6

The Church in Philadelphia

And to the angel of the church in Philadelphia write; These things saith He that is holy, He that is true; He that hath the key of David, He that openeth, and no man shutteth; and shutteth, and no man openeth; I know thy works: behold, I have set before thee an open door, and no man can shut it: for thou hast a little strength, and hast kept my word, and hast not denied my name. Behold, I will make them of the synagogue of Satan, which say they are Jews, and are not, but do lie; behold, I will make them to come and worship before thy feet, and to know that I have loved thee. Because thou has kept the word of my patience, I also will keep thee from the hour of temptation, which shall come upon all the world, to try them that dwell upon the earth. Behold, I come quickly: hold that fast which thou hast, that no man take thy crown. Him that overcometh will I make a pillar in the temple of my God, and he shall go no more out: and I will write upon him the name of my God, and the name of the city of my God, which is new Jerusalem, which cometh down out of heaven from my God: and I will write upon him my new name. He that hath an ear, let him hear what the Spirit saith unto the churches (Rev. 3:7-13).

We now come to *Philadelphia*, which passes without a reproof falling from the lips of Christ. Smyrna was the other Church in which Christ saw no fault. He looked upon them in His own righteousness; and even the eyes of Him, whose eyes are like unto flaming fire, saw nothing to blame; and it is exceedingly remarkable that these two are yet standing. Ephesus left her first love, and the corn is now growing upon its ruins; and there is but one Christian in the village, at one of the extremities where Ephesus was; but Smyrna and Philadelphia yet stand. It is very remarkable to see from these two, that *whosoever keeps the word of Christ, He will keep them*. Both the Churches were suffering, and were yet to suffer persecutions. Smyrna was the place where there were those who said they were Jews, and were not but were of the synagogue of Satan; and Christ said unto them, 'Fear none of those things which thou shalt suffer.' And in Philadelphia there were those who said they were Jews, and were not, but did lie.

In Philadelphia there are 2,000 inhabitants, and 800 professed Christians; there are the remains of twenty old churches, and there are five in which divine service is conducted. Whoso keepeth the word of Christ, He will keep them. You have heard of the infidel Gibbon; he says, 'Philadelphia is still erect – a column in a scene of ruins.' Even the infidel gives testimony to the word of Christ.

The character Christ takes to Himself here. 'These things saith He that is holy, He that is true, He that hath the key of David, He that openeth and no man shutteth; and shutteth, and no man openeth.'

This seems to be taken from the vision in the first chapter, when John was in the Spirit on the Lord's day, and heard behind him a great voice, as of a trumpet. He says, 'And I turned to see the voice that spake with me. And being turned, I saw seven golden candlesticks. And in the midst of the seven candlesticks, one like unto the Son of Man, clothed with a garment down to the foot, and girt about the paps with a golden girdle;' that is, 'He that is true:' and then, at the fourteenth verse, 'His head and His hairs were white like wool, as white as snow; and His eyes were as a flame of fire.' It is to show the purity of Christ, that is, 'He that is holy.' And in the eighteenth verse, 'I am He that liveth, and was dead; and, behold, I am alive for evermore, Amen; and have the keys of hell and of death.' That is, 'He that hath the key of David, He that openeth and no man shutteth; and shutteth, and no man openeth.'

Ours is a holy Saviour. I have known people who cannot come to God, but who think they can come to Christ; they think that He is an indulgent Saviour, and that He will pass over some little things. Oh no! Christ is holy, *He cannot bear any sin*; if He could have borne with it, He would not have come and died; and if He could have borne with it, we might have been taken to His bosom, without Him offering Himself. But He cannot bear sin, He is a holy Saviour. It is true, Christ is anxious that you should be saved, but God is anxious too. Come to Jesus, and come to the Father. Father, Son, and Spirit so loved the world as to give up Christ to die for sinners. Jesus Christ is a true Saviour; 'if it were not so, I would have told you.' He would have told you. Christ could have no end in saying what was not true; come freely, boldly, to Him – He is true.

Are there any anxious, awakened souls here, who would fain take Christ as their Saviour? Now you may take Him; you may rest upon Him; it is He who giveth rest; you may build upon this foundation, for He is complete, He is infinite, He is a rock.

And He 'hath the key of David.' The meaning of this you will find explained in Isaiah 22, from the fifteenth verse to the end. 'Thus saith the Lord God of Hosts, Go, get thee unto this treasurer even unto Shebna, which is over the house, and say,' etc.

This was a message sent to Shebna, the treasurer of the king's palace, to tell him that that office was to be taken from him, that he was to be carried into captivity, that it was to be given over to Eliakim, who was to have the key upon his shoulder. It is meant, that the Levitical priesthood was to be taken into captivity; and Eliakim is typical of Him who was indeed to be a nail in a sure place, and on whom everything was to hang, and on whose shoulder was to be put the key of David, *even Jesus*, of whom it is written,

Unto us a Child is born, unto us a Son is given; and the government shall be upon His shoulder; and His name shall be called Wonderful, Counsellor, the Mighty God, the Everlasting Father, the Prince of Peace.

The key used in those days, and what is still used in Egypt, was not like the key we use. It was the shape of a reaping-hook, the shape of the constellation of stars in the heavens that is like a reaping-hook; it was a large key, made of wood; it was carried on the shoulder, and all the bolts and bars were within, and the key was put into the inside, and opened them there.

It is said in the Song of Solomon, 'My Beloved put in His hand by the hole of the door.' The chief man of a household carried on his shoulder a silver or ivory key; Christ has the key on His shoulder; He has the key of grace, He has the key of providence, He has the key of glory, He has the keys of hell and of death; He is Head over all things to the Church.

He has the key of *Grace*; for He comes, and stands at the door of the heart, and opens the bars. Now, how often, how long has He stood at your hearts! – even until His head was filled with dew, and His locks with the drops of the night. There are some of you whose heart is all bolts and bars; and you are determined not to

72

let Christ in. There is the bar of the love of sin; the bar of pride, of vanity; the bar of the love of the world; the bar of the fear of man, the fear of your companions; but if Christ were only to use the key of grace, all the bolts and bars would fly open. Now, may He reveal Himself unto you, all full, all free, all gracious – a Divine Saviour!

Christ has another key, the key of *Providence*. Sometimes you feel your afflictions to be many; that the door is shut, that you cannot get out. But Jesus has got the key; He can make even the wrath of man to praise Him, and the remainder of wrath can He restrain. Oh, trust Him! 'All power is given unto me in heaven and in earth.' For example, we are building in this town new churches; and we want ministers, and we are apt to fear that we may not succeed; but let us trust Christ; let us go forward in strength; let us go forward in power; let us go forward in simple faith, looking unto Jesus.

And Christ has the key of *Glory*. When a devoted servant of Christ dies, some people say, How mysterious are the ways of God! They cry out, 'My father, my father, the chariots of Israel, and the horsemen thereof!' But Christ does not use the key to open until the very time.

Let us now see the *case of the Church; and, first, Let us look at the character of it.* 'I know thy works: behold, I have set before thee an open door, and no man can shut it; for thou hast a little strength, and hast kept my word, and hast not denied my name.' When travellers used to come from foreign lands to Scotland, they called it Philadelphia, which means love to the brethren. That was the time in Scotland when there was a minister for every thousand people; when every child could read the Bible; and when there was no need of Sabbath schools, for every family was a Sabbath school. We are not a *Philadelphia* now, we are rather a *Laodicea*. Travellers used to say, when they looked upon Scotland, It is like a field of wheat in the midst of lilies – like a palace of silver – a Philadelphia.

But what does Christ say of the Church? 'Behold, I have set before thee an open door, and no man can shut it.' In the Epistle to the Colossians, Paul says, 'Withal praying also for us, that God would open unto us a door of utterance;' it is Christ that opens the door to ministers, and no man can shut it. And in Second Corinthians, Paul says that a door was opened unto him of the Lord. And there is another meaning of this; in the Acts of the

Apostles, in the fourteenth chapter at the twenty-seventh verse, it is written that God opened the door of faith unto the Gentiles. And Christ has set before *you* an open door. It was Christ that laid the foundation-stone of this church, and it is Christ that will put on the top-stone. If any have been awakened here, it is Christ that hath done it; if any have been taught within these walls, it is the Lord; if any have been made to have fuller joy, it is Christ. Let us give Him the glory. He hath set before you an open door, and though many would be anxious to shut it, yet no man can shut it.

'For thou hast a little strength, and hast kept my word, and hast not denied my name.' But a *little* strength! We saw last Sabbath that a little faith saves the soul. A grain of mustard seed is very small; and so faith, like a grain of mustard seed, is very small, but it is very precious; a drop of grace is very small, but it is very precious; this little strength is very precious, for it saves the soul. Would that you had this little strength – that ye had this grain of faith! Despise not the day of small things; and when you see anyone who has got little faith, you should not because of this avoid their company; that's not what Christ would do. 'Him that is weak in the faith receive ye, but not to doubtful disputations.' 'Take care that ye offend not one of these little ones. For whosoever shall offend one of these little ones that believe in me, it is better for him that a millstone were hanged about his neck, and he were cast into the sea.' 'And hast kept my word.' If you are united to Jesus, you will love His saying, 'If a man love me, he will keep my words; and my Father will love him, and we will come unto him, and make our abode with him.'

There are *two* reasons that you should have patience. You need patience *if you would keep your souls unto the end*. In your patience possess ye your souls. 'For ye have need of patience, that, after ye have done the will of God, ye might receive the promise.' He that endureth to the end shall be saved, and none else. With full purpose of heart cleave unto the Lord. You need patience, second, *to keep the word concerning the coming of the Lord Jesus*. 'Seeing it is a righteous thing with God to recompense tribulation to them that trouble you; and to you who are troubled rest with us, when the Lord Jesus shall be revealed from heaven with His mighty angels, in flaming fire, taking vengeance on them that know not God, and that obey not the gospel of our Lord Jesus Christ: who shall be punished with everlasting destruction from the presence of the Lord, and from the glory of His power; when He shall come to be glorified in His saints, and to be admired in all them that believe, in that day.' *Let us wait for His appearing.* 'The Lord is not slack concerning His promise, as some men count slackness, but is long-suffering to us-ward, not willing that any should perish but that all should come to repentance. But the day of the Lord will come as a thief in the night; in the which the heavens shall pass away with a great noise, and the elements shall melt with fervent heat, the earth also, and the works that are therein, shall be burned up.' 'And hast not denied my name.' Luke wrote to Theophilus that he might know the certainty of those things wherein he had been instructed. The deeper the roots of a tree take hold of the ground, the more it spreads its branches; the deeper you are grounded into Christ, the bolder you will become. Hold fast by the word of Christ, and then you will not deny His name. Does this character belong to us? The Lord make this spot like a little Philadelphia, in the midst of a wide Sardis.

Notice now the promises. 'Because thou hast kept the word of my patience, I also will keep thee from the hour of temptation, which shall come upon all the world, to try them that dwell upon the earth. Behold, I come quickly: hold that fast which thou hast, that no man take thy crown.' What a glorious promise of Jesus Christ's, that He will keep all them that keep His word! Notice that these searching times will try all those that dwell on the earth. I do not know when these times will be, but I think they must be near. The Lord stands at the door. Christ said 1800 years ago, Behold, I come quickly; and if He said that then surely He may say now, Behold, *I come instantly*.

James Renwick's words just before his death were ominous – something like Christ's. He said, 'There is a time coming when they shall say, Those were happy who died on the scaffold.'

Let us hold fast the word of Christ just *now*; let us have strong faith; and then we shall be kept in those times. See, it will be but a short time; it is but a night; it is but an hour; it is but a moment. 'Come, my people, enter thou into thy chamber, and shut thy doors about thee; hide thyself as it were for a little moment, until the indignation be overpast.' 'His anger endureth but a moment; in His favour is life: weeping may endure for a night, but joy cometh in the morning.' The Father who gave us to

Christ is greater than all; and none shall be able to pluck us out of His hand.

Let us look now at the reward Christ offers. 'Him that overcometh will I make a pillar in the temple of my God, and he shall go no more out: and I will write upon him the name of my God, and the name of the city of my God, which is New Jerusalem, which cometh down out of heaven from my God: and I will write upon him my new name.' I would rather sit at the threshold – I had rather be a doorkeeper in the house of my God, than to dwell in the tents of wickedness.

There were two pillars in Solomon's temple: the one was called Jachin, that is, He shall establish; the other was called Boaz, that is, In it is strength. There are some of you that would be glad to be stones in the temple; but Christ says of some, that He will make them a *pillar*: there are some of you who would be glad if you just *got in*; but Christ says, you *shall go no more out*. 'And I will write upon him the name of my God.' Even here, one says, I am the Lord's; and another calls himself by the name of Jacob; and another subscribes with his hand unto the Lord, and surnames himself by the name of Israel. But then how *surely it shall be done*, when Christ will write upon us the name of His God!

Here we are possessed with the world – with money – possessed with those we love too much, with our friends; but we belong to that city, that city which hath foundations, whose builder and maker is God. It shall be said of us, we are born here: and observe, we shall be nearer to God than we are to the saints; for it is written, that we 'are no more strangers and foreigners, but fellow-citizens with the saints, and of the household of God;' we shall be in the same *city* with the saints, but in the same *house* with God, of the household of God. Is there any other name Christ could write upon us? Is there anything else in heaven or in the earth He could give us? Yes, 'I will write upon him my new name.'

Ah! If the Saviour's name were not written upon us, the name of His God would not be written upon us. We must have Christ's name written upon us here; He must write it upon us with His own hand; and then we shall have God's name written upon us there. Let us have Christ's old name here, which is Emmanuel, the seed of the woman: and then He will write upon us His new name, which is 'KING OF KINGS AND LORD OF LORDS.' We shall share in His *kingdom*, we shall share in His *crown*, we shall share in His *glory*. 'Father, I will that they also, whom Thou hast given me, be with me where I am; that they may behold my glory which Thou hast given me for Thou lovedst me before the foundation of the world.'

Let us *overcome* – is it not worth fighting for? And then Christ shall make us a pillar, and we shall go no more out; and Christ will write upon us the name of His God, and the name of the city of His God, which is New Jerusalem, and He will write upon us His new name.

EXPOSITION 7

The Church in Laodecia

And unto the angel of the church of the Laodiceans write; These things saith the Amen, the faithful and true Witness, the beginning of the creation of God; I know thy works, that thou art neither cold nor hot: I would thou wert cold or hot. So then because thou art lukewarm, and neither cold nor hot, I will spue thee out of my mouth. Because thou sayest, I am rich, and increased with goods, and have need of nothing; and knowest not that thou art wretched, and miserable, and poor, and blind, and naked: I counsel thee to buy of me gold tried in the fire, that thou mayest be rich; and white raiment, that thou mayest be clothed, and that the shame of thy nakedness do not appear; and anoint thine eyes with eyesalve, that thou mayest see. As many as I love, I rebuke and chasten: be zealous therefore, and repent. Behold I stand at the door, and knock: if any man hear my voice, and open the door, I will come in to him, and will sup with him, and he with me. To him that overcometh will I grant to sit with me in my throne, even as I also overcame, and am set down with my Father in His throne. He that hath an ear, let him hear what the Spirit saith unto the churches (Rev 3:14-22).

We now come to the last of the Seven Churches, and the worst; and I do not know what *you* feel, but I am sorry; because there is not any part in the Bible so instructive, so comforting to the children of God, and so fitted to awaken those who are not in Christ; therefore it is that I am sorry that we are now come to the last of the Seven Epistles to the Seven Churches of Asia. Laodicea is interesting, because Paul speaks of it; he says, in the second chapter of Colossians, at the first verse, 'For I would that ye knew what great conflict I have for you, and for them at Laodicea, and for as many as have not seen my face in the flesh.' Again he speaks of them, in the fourth chapter, at the thirteenth verse, 'For I bear him record, that he hath a great zeal for you, and them that are in Laodicea, and them in Hierapolis.' In the year of our Lord 64, Laodicea was overthrown by an earthquake, but it was rebuilt again, and it was much finer than before; there were in it three theatres, and a circus, so large that it held at one time 30,000 people. It was in the year 96 that Christ sent this epistle to them; and in a few years after, Laodicea was overthrown by a second earthquake, buried under its own ruins, and never rose again; and it is now quite uninhabited, quite desolate. One of the last travellers that was there says that he found Laodicea 'without any inhabitant, except wolves, and jackals, and foxes.' See how true Christ has been to His words to all the Seven Churches.

The character Christ takes to Himself here. 'These things saith the Amen, the faithful and true Witness, the beginning of the creation of God.' The Amen! This was Christ's favourite word. Verily, verily; it means in the Hebrew, to be true. Christ is true to all He says; 'All the promises of God in Him are yea, and in Him amen, unto the glory of God by us.' There are some of you who wish you had the Spirit. Now Christ is true, and He has said, 'I will pray the Father, and He shall give you another Comforter, that He may abide with you for ever; even the Spirit of truth: whom the world cannot receive, because it seeth Him not,

85

neither knoweth Him; but ye know Him, because He dwelleth with you, and shall be in you.' And again, 'I will send Him unto you; for though He tarry, yet wait for Him, for He will come, and will not tarry.' The promise may be long delayed, but never comes too late. Christ makes two kinds of promises: *threatening* ones and *comforting* ones. Now there are some of you whose only hope is that Christ will not prove true to His words. But He is the Amen. Do you think He will take away that word Amen and put liar instead? Christ will be true to His *threatening* as well as to His *comforting* promises; He is a *Destroyer* as well as a *Saviour* – He is the Amen. It is written, that 'the Lord Jesus shall be revealed from heaven with His mighty angels, in flaming fire, taking vengeance on them that know not God, and that obey not the gospel of our Lord Jesus Christ: who shall be punished with everlasting destruction from the presence of the Lord, and from the glory of His power.'

'The faithful and true Witness.' This means, that Christ bears true testimony; He witnesses true *of our condition*; 'These things are for your sakes, upon whom the ends of the world have come.' Christ never flatters, He tells us our true state; He makes us no better than we are, and no worse. He is Nature's sternest painter, but her best. If Christ were revealed to any of you tonight, you would go away, and say, 'Come, see a man that told me all things that ever I did: is not this the Christ?' And then Christ witnesses true of God; He witnesses of what He hath seen in the bosom of the Father – 'No man hath seen God at any time; the only begotten Son, which is in the bosom of the Father, He hath declared Him.' 'We speak that we do know, and testify that we have seen.'

Christ testifies what is in the heart of God towards sinners. How willing He is that they should be saved, because He knows it, and has seen it. 'Come unto me, all ye that labour and are heavy laden, and I will give you rest.' *There is no rest for the soul like being in the love of God* – that is rest. Not until then can it say, 'Return unto thy rest, O my soul; for the Lord hath dealt bountifully with thee.' And Christ witnesses *about Himself*, 'Though I bear record of myself, yet my record is true.' He bears witness of His love; He bears witness of His dying; He bears witness of His steadfastness, setting His face like a flint; and He witnesses that He has got the tongue of the learned, that He should know how to speak a word in season to him that is weary.

'The beginning of the creation of God.' It should rather be rendered *author* or *prince*. 'In the beginning was the Word, and the Word was with God, and the Word was God.' It was Christ that set the sun and the moon to run their golden race, and placed the stars with their lights of fire; it was Christ that gathered the earth together, and formed the rivers. It makes creation sweeter, it makes the trees sweeter, to know that all is the work of Christ; and it makes us more sure of the world on which we tread: we might be afraid that an earthquake would come, but we know that nothing shall happen but what is the will of Christ. He toucheth the hills, and they smoke. Christ seems to have taken this character, 'The beginning of the creation of God,' to Laodicea: just as much as to say, I sent the first earthquake; and if you do not repent, I am able to send another.

Let us look at the character of the Church.

> I know thy works, that thou art neither cold nor hot; I would thou wert cold or hot. So then because thou art lukewarm, and neither cold nor hot, I will spue thee out of my mouth. Because thou sayest, I am rich, and increased with goods, and have need of nothing; and knowest not that thou art wretched, and miserable, and poor, and

blind, and naked: I counsel thee to buy of me gold tried in the fire, that thou mayest be rich; and white raiment, that thou mayest be clothed, and that the shame of thy nakedness do not appear; and anoint thine eyes with eyesalve, that thou mayest see.'

The Church had two peculiarities; *lukewarmness* and *self-righteousness*. Christ has a word suited to every part of the character.

Let us take the first of these, *lukewarmness*. There are three characters spoken of:

First, the *cold*. Who are the cold? Those who are frozen, those who are icicles, those who give and who take no heat. A dead body is cold and motionless; the hands are clammy, and the cold dew of death is on the forehead. And a cold, dead soul is far worse. Gallio cared for none of these things. Are there not many Gallios among us; those who care for none of these things? No wonder that there is so much corruption, when there are so many dead souls. The wonder is, that the children of God are kept at all; if it were not for the Spirit, they would soon have no life.

Second, the *lukewarm*. Who are the lukewarm? Those who have the form of godliness, but who deny the power thereof; those who are lovers of pleasure more than lovers of God; those who are faithful at ordinances, who come every Sabbath to church, who are faithful in the world, those who are almost persuaded to be Christians. Now, this is what Christ hates most of all – He would rather have you to be cold or hot, than to be lukewarm. Are there not some of you who mock at such a thing as *warmth in religion*, and call it *enthusiasm*; at having affection to Christ? Are there not some of you who do not love to hear that word asked, 'Simon, son of Jonas, lovest thou me more than these?', who do not like to hear of a broken spirit, who do not like to hear of the forgiveness of sins? *You* are the lukewarm; turn ye, turn ye, why will ye die? 'Woe unto thee, Chorazin! Woe unto thee, Bethsaida! For if the mighty works which were done in you had been done in Tyre and Sidon, they would have repented long ago in sackcloth and ashes,' etc. Those who almost got to the gate of heaven, *but who have never come to Christ*, will have a deeper place in hell than profligate sinners.

Third, the *hot*. Who are the hot? The dear children of God, those whose hearts are burning with love to God, and with love to the brethren; they are like the Seraphim, always burning. Christ baptizes us with the Holy Ghost and with fire.

Let us see now the other part of the character – self-righteousness. Lukewarmness and pride always go together. If there are any of you who have been offended at what I have said tonight, *you* are the very persons; the self-righteous, the *moral* people. There is *one sweet thing* here – Christ never threatens only; after the threatening comes a *counsel*, and after that a *promise*. 'God resisteth the proud, but giveth grace unto the humble.' Oh the love that is in the heart of Christ! He says, 'If any man thirst, let him come unto me and drink.'

You think you are rich, and increased in goods; and it is true that if to be rich is to have long prayers, then you are increased in goods. But see what God says in the first chapter of Isaiah, at the eleventh verse:

To what purpose is the multitude of your sacrifices unto me? saith the LORD: I am full of the burnt offerings of rams, and the fat of fed beasts; and I delight not in the blood of bullocks, or of lambs, or of he-goats. When ye come to appear before me, who hath required this at your hand, to tread my courts? Bring no more vain oblations; incense is an abomination unto me; the new moons and sabbaths, the calling of assemblies, I cannot away with; it is iniquity, even the solemn meeting.

You do not know the misery of being out of Christ; you think you are rich, although you are poor; you are a beggar, all your righteousnesses are as filthy rags; and 'all things are naked and open unto the eyes of Him with whom we have to do.'

When you go home tonight, perhaps some of you will say, what could the minister mean by telling us that we are miserable, when we are quite happy? and what could he mean by telling us that we are poor, and that we are blind, when we see quite well? But this is just because you do not know; and Christ knew that, for He says, Thou *knowest* not that thou art wretched, etc.

And yet observe, that although you are so proud, Christ is meek and lowly: although you be so proud, He counsels you, He advises you, but then you do not want it. Now, whether are you or Christ to be the wiser? He advises you to buy of Him 'gold tried in the fire'. All *Christ's gold has been in the fire, all put into the fire of God's anger*, the fine gold of heaven. And He counsels you to buy of Him 'white raiment' – raiment such as no fuller on earth can white them. Now may God put this within you, that, after all, *Christ may be right*!

Does He offer anything else? Yes. I see

everything in the Lord Jesus; this eye-salve is the oil of gladness, the Spirit of the Lord Jesus. Now, if Christ were to anoint you with this tonight, that would lighten your eyes; you would go away saying, 'One thing I know, that whereas I was blind, now I see.'

Now let us look at Jesus' promise. Christ was like a merchant in the market-place advising you to buy of Him; and now you have gone home – it is suppertime – and He follows you, wishing still that you buy His wares; and He says, 'Behold, I stand at the door, and knock: if any man hear my voice, and open the door, I will come in to him, and will sup with him, and he with me.' Or it should rather be, *I have been standing* at the door, *and am standing still!*

There is not a more touching passage than this in the whole Bible. Jesus has been long standing at the door of your hearts, and He knocks at it in the *Bible* – every time you read it, that is Christ knocking; and He knocks at your door by *godly friends,* by *godly parents*; and He knocks by the *words of ministers,* the words that come into your mind of those ministers, *who have now gone to their rest, and rise now enjoying their crown*: and Christ knocks by *providences* that have met you in your family; by lost friends; by the fairest flower of your flock being taken from you. And you thought it was a rude hand, *but it was Christ's*; it was Christ, who wants to reveal Himself to you, who wants to be a Saviour to you; it was Christ, who wants to be revealed *in* you, and wants to manifest Himself unto you, in another way than He doth unto the world. And He has knocked at your hearts, *in these Seven Epistles*; the Lord has been in this place, although you knew it not; He has stood until His head is filled with dew, and His locks with the drops of the night. He has pleaded by *His blood and by His tears*. Now, if you would hear Christ's voice, and open the door, what does the Lord Jesus say He would do? 'I will come in to him, and will sup with him, and he with me.'

> Judas saith unto Him, 'Lord, how is it that Thou wilt manifest Thyself unto us, and not unto the world?' Jesus answered and said unto him, 'If a man love me, he will keep my words; and my Father will love him, and we will come unto him and make our abode with him.'

How happy *to have Christ sit down with you at every meal*! How happy to eat bread with

Christ! And now we have come to the last of the Seven Churches of Asia, and we must leave them; and observe, *I take you all to witness, that the last word of Christ to you was a word of kindness – a word of mercy*: 'Behold, I stand at the door, and knock; if any man hear my voice, and open the door, I will come in to him, and will sup with him, and he with me.'